Gloria Whelan

Eerdmans Books for Young Readers

Grand Rapids, Michigan

Copyright © 1994 by Gloria Whelan
Published 1994 by Eerdmans Books for Young Readers an
imprint of Wm. B. Eerdmans Publishing Co.
255 Jefferson Ave. S.E., Grand Rapids, Michigan 49503

Printed in the United States of America

06 05 04 03   7 6 5 4 3

Library of Congress Cataloging-in-Publication Data

Whelan, Gloria.
That wild berries should grow: the diary of a summer /
Gloria Whelan.
p.   cm.
Summary: Elsa dreads spending the summer at her grandparents'
house on Lake Huron, but she discovers the excitement of nature
and the richness of friendship.

ISBN 0-8028-5254-8

[1. Summer—Fiction.   2. Nature—Fiction.
3. Friendship—Fiction.]   I. Title.
PZ7.W5718Th   1994
[Fic]—dc20   93-41106
CIP
AC

www.eerdmans.com

To
Jacqueline

The City

They tell me,
"The country will be good for you,"
and send me like a package
to my grandparents' cottage.

On the highway
the car is an eraser,
friends and houses disappear.

Driving all day,
country is what's left
when everything else
is taken away.

We live in Detroit. Even though it's 1933 and the Depression, the city is alive with things to do. The sidewalks are crowded with people. The air has the rich smell of the buses and cars that rush by our apartment. The Packard automobile factory is just down the street. Before the Depression, when all the people lost their jobs, the factory windows flickered day and night with a wonderful blue-green light. It made you think witchery was going on inside.

There are six apartments in our building. We aren't the only members of our family who live there. When the Depression came, all of Grandpapa's children moved into his apartment building because they couldn't afford to keep their own houses. Our apartment is on the first floor. My Aunt Edna and Uncle Tom live across the way from us. Aunt Fritzie and Uncle Tim live over us on the second floor, and Uncle John and Aunt Emmy live across from them.

We're all supposed to pay rent to my grandfather, but none of us do. My uncles have lost their jobs. Only my Aunt Edna works. She is a schoolteacher. When my grandfather comes to collect the rents, all he gets is oatmeal cookies at our place, date and nut squares from Aunt Ella, store-bought cookies from Aunt Edna, and a big kiss from Aunt Fritzie. My grandfather never complains.

The good thing about having so many aunts and uncles under the same roof is that if one of them gets bored with me there is always another aunt and uncle. The bad thing is that they don't have any children of their own, so I am always being divided up.

I love the city. Before I got sick, my mom would put on her best dress, her hat with the veil, and her white gloves. I would wear my organdy dress and my crocheted gloves. We'd take the bus downtown. Holding hands, we'd wander through Hudson's Department Store—all twelve floors. We never bought anything. It was the Depression, and we didn't have money to spend. Still, as long as we were in the store we could pretend that anything we wanted was ours.

My parents took me to the Art Institute, where you walk through a great hall lined with the armor that knights used to wear. Besides all the pictures there is a room with mummies, which are dead people all bandaged up. On Sunday afternoons, if we had enough money for gasoline, we would join the long lines of automobiles snaking down East Grand Boulevard on their way to Belle Isle for picnics and canoeing. There is always something to see and do in the city.

Usually when I saw my grandparents it was in their big old-fashioned house in the city, but twice I had gone with my mother and father for short visits to Greenbush, where my grandparents had a summer cottage on Lake Huron. I remembered two things about those visits. There was nothing to do, and the huge lake you couldn't see to the end of was everywhere you looked. I was so relieved when it was time to climb into the car and leave that I hardly noticed my grandparents waving good-bye, a sad look on their faces.

I never guessed that one day I would be sent away from the city to spend a whole summer with my grandparents. It happened because I got sick. First I had a sore throat. Then the doctor listened to my heart. He shook his head and said I had to go to bed for five months—half of fifth grade. I lost January, February, March, April, and May. There was nothing to do but read books and write poems.

The poems happened because of the get-well letters my teacher made my classmates write to me. One of the letters was a poem. It was a dumb one written by Lucille Macken, who thought she was so smart:

Roses are red,
Violets are blue,
Because you're sick,
I feel sorry for you.

I was sure I could write better poems. So I tried. I didn't think they were very good, but my mom saw them and said they were excellent—her favorite word for something that's not bad; she's an optimist.

Just when I could finally get out of bed, my parents sat me down.

"We have a wonderful surprise for you," Mom said. Surprises are someone else's idea of what you would like. "The doctor feels you need fresh air." She was trying to look happy, but it wasn't working.

I began to worry. I knew the only place you find fresh air is where there is nothing else.

Dad said, "You're going to spend the whole summer in

Greenbush with your grandmama and grandpapa at their cottage on Lake Huron."

"What do you mean the *whole* summer?" I guessed what my dad must mean. Three months. Thirty days times three. Ninety days times twenty-four hours. There would be thousands of hours. I would hate every one of them. I'd be far away from my friends. There would be nothing to do in the country. That big lake would be there ready to swallow me up.

Besides, there was my grandmama. We often go to my grandparents' home in the city. But I am always a little afraid of Grandmama. She seems sour and prickly. You have to think ahead about what you say to her or you'll get a tart reply. Now I was going to have to spend the whole summer with her.

"But I'm all better," I pleaded.

"You still have headaches," Dad reminded me.

"No, I don't," I said. I wasn't telling the truth. Sometimes my head felt like someone was careening around inside it with a hammer.

I moped. I sulked. I refused to eat. I cried. I tried temper tantrums. All my parents would say is, "Dr. Kellet thinks a summer in the country will be good for you." Things that are supposed to be good for you usually turn out to be terrible.

There was another reason why I had to spend the summer with my grandparents. My dad is a builder. With the Depression, no one is building anything. Things are so bad that for a couple of days in March all the banks in the country closed down. Every morning my father shines his shoes and brushes his hat. He whistles "Row, Row, Row Your Boat" while he brushes and shines. I think it's for good luck. Mom presses his trousers, the steam from her damp pressing cloth clouding the kitchen. As Dad leaves he always says, "I've got a feeling today is my lucky day." At supper time when he comes home he just looks at Mom and shakes his head. After I'm in bed at night I can hear their worried whispers in the next room.

Little by little the nice things we had, presents from my dad to my mom or from my grandparents to us, have disappeared. Mom's silver dresser set and even her sewing machine were sold for money to buy groceries. I know the special food they buy to make me healthy is expensive. That makes me feel so bad I can hardly eat it. So it just gets wasted, which is even worse. "In the country you'll have wonderful things to eat, Elsa," Mom said. And I knew that was the other reason I was being sent away.

So on June 5 we left for Greenbush and my grandparents' cottage. Dad took a day off. I think he was sort of relieved to have a reason not to have to face all those people who don't want him to build things. Just before we piled into the car, Mother said, "Here's a present for you." It was wrapped up in the pretty paper and ribbon she saved from my dad's birthday present to her. I was still sulking, but except for Christmas and my birthday I'd never had a present, so it was hard pretending I wasn't excited. I unwrapped the present carefully to save the paper. There was a notebook with flowers all over the cover and empty pages.

"It's for your poems," Mom said.

We got in the car and headed for the country. I watched through the car windows as the buildings got smaller and the trees got larger. Where there should have been houses there were only fields. I opened my new notebook. It's hard to write when you're bumping around in a car, but I wrote a poem.

The Country

Homesick
under blank sky,
empty land around me,
I want the city
where tall buildings knock clouds,
lock arms to keep back
the boring fields.

We drove for hours until finally we got to the town, which doesn't seem like a real town at all. It only has one long street with a few small stores on either side. A little way out of Greenbush we turned onto a narrow road. At the end of the road, perched on a high bank, I saw my grandparents' white and green cottage. Neat rows of trees march across the yard, and flowers spill over the walk.

Behind the cottage, the blue lake goes on forever.

My grandparents hurried out to meet the car. They both came from Germany. That was a long time ago, but they still talk with a German accent. Grandpapa is short, with a round face, round blue eyes, and a neatly trimmed mustache. Grandmama is a large, square woman, with green slanty eyes and a pile of brown hair coiled on top of her head. She would be pretty if it weren't for the tight way she holds her lips.

From the outside, the two-storied cottage looks no different from any other cottage. Inside, the cottage is like an art museum. My grandpapa is an artist and decorates houses for a living. Around the dining room walls he's painted bunches of grapes and bowls of fruit and jugs of wine. Fish swim on the bathroom walls, and little angels fly up the stairway. Sometimes I have the feeling that if I stand still I might have something painted on me.

Mom spent most of the evening telling Grandmama what I was supposed to eat. "Broths and vegetables and fruits," Mother said. "Healthy things."

"And lots of rest," Dad said. "Elsa needs a nap in the afternoon and an early bedtime." I'd spent so much time resting in the last five months that I hated the very sight of a bed. It's bad enough to be sick, but it's worse if you're an only child. You have your parents' and all your aunts' and uncles' full attention. It's like you're swimming around in a goldfish bowl and you're the only goldfish.

Grandpapa saw the look on my face and winked at me.

Grandmama said, "We're busy here. There's not going

to be time for a lot of pampering."

The rest of the evening they talked about how bad things were in Germany. They didn't like the new government that had been elected there. My grandparents were worried about friends of theirs who lived in Berlin. "We write to them," Grandpapa said, "but we wonder if our letters will make trouble for them."

In the morning, before my parents left to go back home, my mom took me aside. "You're not to worry about your grandmama's 'ways,'" she said, and she sighed. "Your grandmama means well. Watch her hands and you'll understand her better."

Before I could ask her what she meant, it was time to say good-bye. Mom and Dad drove off, turning around every inch of the way to wave. When their car disappeared around a bend in the road, I waited for my grandparents to tell me what to do, just like my parents always do. My parents don't exactly tell me, but when they start a sentence with "Why don't you . . . ," I know they expect me to do what they suggest. They suggest all the time.

My grandparents put on matching straw hats. Grandmama said she had to weed her garden. Grandpapa said he was going to prune the apple trees. There were no suggestions for me, so I followed my grandpapa to the orchard.

The trunk of each tree was painted white. "It's a special paint that helps keep away the bugs," Grandpapa said. "These are apple trees: Jonathan and Rome Beauty, and my Spitzenburg just like we had in the old country.

These are peach trees: Mayflower and Elberta and Red Haven. Over there are pear trees: Russetts and Bosc and Bartlett, and the plum trees, Damson and Mirabelle." He said the names as though he were introducing me to old friends.

Along one side of the orchard is a sort of bank that drops off. When I looked over the edge, all I could see was a spooky-looking tangle of trees and bushes. "What's that?" I asked.

"That's the gully," he said. "When we have a heavy rain the gully takes a bite out of our land."

"Gully," I repeated. From my grandpapa's explanation it sounded like an animal. I save words like some people save stamps or baseball cards. That's a keeper, I thought, repeating it to myself.

I wandered over to Grandmama. All I could see of her was her straw hat sticking up. She was deep in a tangle of flowers, weeding. There were red and yellow and blue flowers, as if someone were trying out all the colors in a box of crayons. "Grandmama, what kind of flowers are they?" I asked politely.

She looked up at me, a little cross at being interrupted. "Cosmos, black-eyed Susans, pansies, lilies, larkspur, daisies, phlox, poppies, and *Vergiss-nicht-mein*, forget-me-nots." I couldn't remember all the names, so I picked "forget-me-nots" to keep. "Gully, Mirabelle, forget-me-nots," I said to myself.

I saw that my grandparents were leaving me on my own. If I were in the city I could have done a hundred things: walk to the dime store and wander up and down the aisles, call my friends, bother my aunts and uncles. Just sitting on the apartment porch and watching traffic was more interesting than being here in this empty place.

There was nothing beyond the orchard but fields, so I wandered around to the front yard. A walk leads from the front of the cottage to wooden steps. The steps go down a steep bank to a wide beach and the lake. There were a few fishing boats out on the lake and, almost farther than I could see, a long freighter. Waves splashed against the beach, making a gulping sound. My dad had taught me to swim at Belle Isle, but the lake was so different—so big and rough. I felt as though the big lake were an enormous fish waiting to swallow me. I wasn't ready to go down those steps.

The sounds I heard were strange ones. An orange and black bird, almost too bright to be real, was singing in an apple tree. The wind rattled the leaves of a birch tree. I missed the squeal of brakes and the honking of horns. I missed my friends, even Lucille Macken. I missed the city.

Greenbush

The children
who live in this town
all year round

stand in front
of the drugstore
close as the slats
in a picket fence.

I can go in—
because they let me.

We eat our meals in the kitchen on a table covered with a blue-and-white checked cloth. Lunch today was strange. Grandpapa had a huge bowl of sliced cucumbers with sour cream. Grandmama and I had potatoes that had been fried with bacon and onion. I wanted to say that my mother doesn't allow me to have fried foods, but I thought that might not be polite. Besides, the potatoes were buttery and crisp, and I was hungry. For dessert there were slices of sunshine cake with thick lemon frosting.

It had been months and months since I had seen so much food. I wasn't surprised, though. We had our Thanksgiving dinners and Christmas dinners at my grandparents' home. Grandmama would heap food onto our plates and urge us to eat. I think she knew that there often wasn't much to eat in our own homes. When we were ready to go home she always had big packages of leftovers for us to take with us.

I ate a lot, in spite of the fact that all my grandparents talked about during lunch was worms and rusts and beetles and mildews. These were all things that killed fruit trees dead. You had to get them before they got the trees. The orchard looked peaceful, but I learned there was war out there.

Even the flowers seemed to be in danger. I helped Grandmama with the dishes. When she was finished, she took her dishpan of soapsuds and threw them over her roses. "Keeps the bugs away," she said. Then she began gathering weeds from the lawn.

"What are you doing?" I asked.

"The dandelions are tender this time of year and make a good salad," she said. "The sorrel will make a good sauce. Taste it."

I chewed some of the green leaves, and they tasted sour in a nice way.

No one ever told me to go to my room and rest. But now that I could do what I liked, there was nothing to do. "Is there a city near here?" I asked Grandpapa that afternoon.

"A city?" he repeated in a puzzled voice.

"You know. Stores and buildings and things."

"Why would you want a city when you have the lake and the trees and the flowers?" I guess he saw the disappointed look on my face because then he said, "There is Greenbush."

"Could I walk there?" I asked. I wanted to find someone my own age to play with. I didn't want to spend the summer with no one but my old grandparents.

"Yah, it's no more than a mile." He showed me the direction to take. He didn't say that he would have to come with me. Instead, he said, "Stop at the post office and pick up the mail."

The road into Greenbush curves along fields and past scattered houses and into the small town, which is on a kind of hill. At the bottom of the hill, the lake was watching me as though it had followed me into town. On one side of Greenbush's main street is Crosby's Drug Store, a library, a bank, and the post office. On the other side of the street is Foley's Grocery Store and a store with a sign that says "Hatton's: Furniture and Undertaker." That's all. It's like someone started to build the town from blocks and then ran out of blocks.

At our post office in the city you just mail your letters and leave. At this post office people stood around talking to one another and to the lady behind the counter. She knew everyone. She even knew me. Before I could say a word she handed me some letters for my grandparents. I was so surprised that I blurted out, "How did you know I was me?"

"It's a small town," she said. Then she added, "And you're all gussied up."

"Gussied" was a word to keep. When I looked at the little town I thought of what my father used to say: "All dressed up and no place to go."

Mother had given me twenty-five cents for summer spending money. I had brought a nickel of that along. I walked up the main street to Crosby's Drug Store, where some boys and girls were talking and laughing together. They were wearing shorts and faded shirts, and they were barefoot. The postmistress was right. I was all gussied up. I had on a dress with a sash tied into a big bow and white socks with patent leather slippers.

I knew I looked funny to them because they stared at me while I walked up the steps and into the drugstore. When I came out with my candy bar, a boy with red hair and watery blue eyes called out, "Look, it's Shirley Temple!" I could hear their giggles all the way down the street. I was so mad I decided I would rather die than be friends with anyone who lived in the town of Greenbush.

As soon as I got home I dug some shorts out of my

suitcase. I took off my shoes and socks. I wasn't allowed to go barefoot in the city, but when I came downstairs my grandparents didn't seem to notice. "The woman in the post office knew who I was," I told them.

"Yah, she knows most things, and what she doesn't know the banker knows, and what he doesn't know Crosby in the drugstore knows," Grandpapa said.

"And what Crosby doesn't know Hatton, the undertaker, finds out," Grandmama added.

"There were some children standing in front of the drugstore, and they laughed at me because of what I was wearing."

"You can find unkindness everywhere," Grandmama said. "Carl, tell Elsa what happened to us when her mother was young."

I could see that Grandpapa didn't want to tell the story, but he took a deep breath and said, "It was during the war in 1917. America was on one side of the war and Germany was on the other. There was a shortage of gasoline in America, so they made a law that you couldn't drive your car on Sundays. One day I took very sick. I knew that I must go at once to a hospital."

"I ran to get our friend, Mr. Ladamacher, to drive us," Grandmama said. "It was a Sunday, when you weren't supposed to drive, but Mr. Ladamacher said, 'Never mind. It is an emergency.' As we drove through town on the way to the hospital people called out, 'The Germans are disobeying the law. They want America to lose the war.' "

Grandpapa said, "But we were Americans, and our son Tom was in the American army."

"They didn't care," Grandmama said. "They threw stones at our car. One of the stones broke a window."

"Gussie, that was a long time ago. We should forget it. Now we have many friends in the town. Why should we frighten Elsa?"

It's hard for Grandmama to forget things that make her unhappy, but Grandpapa is like his paintings, which are all bright colors.

The Screen Porch

A room,
not outside,
not in,
but holding me
in airy
captivity,
while all about
birds
and bees
fly free,
and caged,
I look out.

O ne day I got a letter from Lucille Macken.

Saturday afternoon we got to go to the movies. They had tap dancing lessons first and then an hour of cartoons and two serials and a double feature. We were at the movies for five and a half hours!!! I stopped at the dime store afterwards and bought a Tangee lipstick!!!

I hate it when someone uses a lot of exclamation points. I hate it when someone tells you what a good time they had someplace when you weren't there.

There was nothing to do but read. I spent a lot of time on the screen porch, curled up on the swing with a book. I felt safer on the porch than I did outdoors. Outdoors there were ants, spiders, beetles, mosquitoes, fish flies, ladybugs, bumblebees, hornets, caterpillars, worms, snakes, toads, mice, and chipmunks. Something was always buzzing around my head or crawling up my leg. I didn't understand why there had to be so many extra things.

From the porch I could keep an eye on the lake. One day it is quiet, smooth, shiny, and bright blue like my mother's good silk dress. Another day it is dark green and noisy, with foaming waves that eat up the shore. You can't depend on the lake.

If my parents were here they would ask, "Why don't you go down and splash around in the lake?" My grandparents let me do as I like. Sometimes when they come upon me suddenly they seem surprised to find me here.

What they have noticed is that I've been eating a lot. "Soon you will be less *spärlich*," my grandmama said. That means thin. And the hammer in my head has stopped. No more headaches. That doesn't mean I like it here though. One day at lunch I complained, "There's nothing to do."

My grandparents looked up from their angel food cake as if they couldn't believe what they heard. "You must get outside more. You can't just stay like a captive in that screen porch," Grandpapa said. "You can help us in the garden."

"Elsa must have her own garden," Grandmama told him.

That afternoon Grandpapa dug up a part of the field at the end of the orchard. All the grass and weeds disappeared, leaving a large square of bare earth. He wiped the sweat from his forehead and said, "There you are, Elsa. Now you'll have something to do." He grinned at me, his eyes very blue in his tanned skin, his gray hair tousled from the breeze that blows off the lake.

Grandmama said, "What do you want to grow?" She held out packets of seeds with pictures of vegetables and flowers on them. I would have liked to grow just flowers, but then I remembered how Mother would look longingly at the fresh vegetables in the store. She would study the prices, and then with a shake of her head she would choose carrots or cabbage, which were the cheapest vegetables to buy. I imagined filling bags full of vegetables from my garden and taking them home to her. I guess I had some idea that the vegetables would grow overnight, because I'd decided that I was going to find some way to get back home. And soon.

I picked out beans and tomatoes and lettuce and peas. Then, because I liked their bright colors and their name, I pointed to a package of snapdragons. Grandmama showed me how to stretch a string from one end of my garden to the other to make straight rows. The seeds were so tiny that you could hardly see them. I put them one by one into the ground and patted them down. The earth felt warm under my hand. Grandpapa filled the tin sprinkling can from the rain barrel and carried it to my garden for me. As I sprinkled, the water turned the ground a deep rich color. I could feel the seeds drinking.

After the garden was planted I went back to the screen porch, but every hour or so I hurried out to the garden to see if anything had come up. Finally Grandmama told me that it would take a couple of weeks. I was sure that in a couple of weeks I would find a way to get back to the city. In a couple of weeks I'd be at the movies with Lucille Macken and maybe even wearing lipstick. Someone else would have to take care of my garden.

Night

In the city the rule was:
come home when
the street lights go on.
In the country
I know it is night
when overhead
the white patches
disappear from the wings
of the nighthawks
and the whippoorwill
makes his rounds boasting
he can stay out
as late as he pleases.

After dinner tonight I went out to check my garden. Even though it's been nearly a week since I planted it, nothing seemed to be happening. But when I dug up one of the beans I had planted, I saw a sprout with two tiny leaves sticking out. I stuck it back in the ground, hoping I hadn't killed it.

I stood at the edge of the orchard and looked out over the fields that lay between me and the road that led back to the city. As the sun began going down, things got quieter and quieter. The birds disappeared, except for some black-and-white birds that my grandparents said were nighthawks. They flew up so high in the sky that you could hardly see them, and then they dropped down until you thought they would crash into the ground. Instead, just in time, they swooped up again. As it grew dark there were no sounds but the crickets chirping and the call of the whippoorwill. Nighthawks and whippoorwills. The names sounded sad to me.

I missed the sounds of the city: the cars screeching past our apartment, and my friends calling to one another. Lots of children live up and down our street. In the early evenings, before I got sick, we would play "Relievo" and "Giant Steps." There were six of us. Every night after dinner we would hurry out of our houses to find each other. Sometimes we would just sit and watch the cars hurry by until the streetlights came on. In the city you never have to listen to silence like you do in the country. There is always something to talk back to you, even if it's just an automobile horn or the squeal of brakes.

The quiet of the country made me nervous, so I hurried back to the cottage before it got dark. Grandmama was sitting in her favorite chair, hemming dishtowels and listening to Caruso records on the Victrola. Caruso is a famous Italian singer who is dead now. Grandpapa was reading the newspaper, shaking his head over what he was reading. "Germany has chosen a dangerous leader. This Hitler is an evil man. We have friends in Germany who will find themselves in trouble. I only hope they can leave before it is too late."

I asked Grandpapa, "Why did you come to America from Germany?"

"*Ach*, over there they wanted everyone to go into the army. They would have sent me to Africa to fight just so they could steal a little more land for themselves. That was not for me."

Grandmama sighed. "But when we came away from Germany we had to leave behind everyone we loved." I thought about my parents and my aunts and uncles and my friends miles away in the city, and I understood what Grandmama felt. Grandmama told me about the *grossen Schiff*, the big boat, that had brought her and Grandpapa to America. "We sailed from the city of Bremerhaven," she said. "My papa and mama and my brothers and sister all came to see us off. As the boat pulled away from the dock my family grew smaller and smaller until I couldn't see them at all. They separated your grandpapa and me. The women had their own cabins and the men had theirs. I was in a stateroom no larger than a closet with four other women, and I knew none of them."

"You became good friends," Grandpapa said. "We could hear you laughing and giggling."

"For the first days we were all seasick. You can't have five women in a closet, all throwing up together, without becoming friends."

Grandpapa laughed. "You should have been in my cabin. Hans Liebig's mother packed a basket for him to take on the ship. The basket was the size of a bathtub. We ate from it for a week: bread, sausages, pickles, cheeses, cakes. We were so busy eating Hans's food we had no time to be seasick."

"Except for the canoes on Belle Isle," I said, "I've never been in a boat."

"Our friend Mr. Ladamacher has a boat," Grandpapa said. "This week we will take you out on the lake fishing."

I wished I hadn't said anything about a boat. I didn't think I wanted to be out on that big lake in a little boat.

Fishing

A chase in the bait box
until my five quick fingers hug
the minnow's slick body,
the flat face, the hook
in and out of the lips,
then overboard and freedom
on a string to tempt
a passing perch. Soon
two prisoners dancing
to a single tune.

Today was our day to go fishing on Mr. Ladamacher's boat. It took forever to load the car. There were straw hats and umbrellas to protect us from the hot sun. There were raincoats in case it should rain. There were cushions to sit on. There were bottles of Grandpapa's homemade root beer packed in ice.

There was also the picnic hamper. Grandmama was up at daybreak making our lunch: sweet and sour potato salad with bacon and green onions, deviled eggs, ham and chicken sandwiches, sugar and molasses and oatmeal cookies. Living in the country seemed to put you closer to food. I wished I could pack some of it up and send it to my parents.

When he saw us unload our car, Mr. Ladamacher shook his head. "My little boat will never hold all of that," he said. But it did. We put on our straw hats and sat on our sweaters and cushions and tucked the food under the seats. Grandpapa and Mr. Ladamacher fished and Grandmama kept handing around food.

At first the boat was close to the shore and I wasn't too worried, but as the shore got farther and farther away, the boat started to feel as small as a thimble bobbing on the lake. Grandpapa saw how scared I looked. To take my mind off the big lake he asked if I wanted to try fishing. He found a pole for me. "Catch yourself a minnow from the pail and put it on the hook." I looked into a pail of quick silvery forms flashing back and forth in the water. My hand closed on one of the silvery darts. I felt the minnow squirm in my hand. Grandpapa showed me how to stick the minnow on a hook. The line went into the water. I watched the minnow disappear into the lake.

I was sitting there feeling awful about the minnow when I felt a tug on the line and let out a scream. "Hang on," Grandpapa said. I reeled in a fish.

Grandmama was pleased. "A nice perch. Big enough for the frying pan." When I put the next minnow on the hook I hardly felt sorry for it at all.

We had the perch for dinner, and they were the best fish I ever tasted. We all went upstairs to bed early. "There's no lullaby like a rocking boat," Grandpapa said.

The quiet followed me all the way up the narrow wooden stairway to my bedroom, where my grandpapa has painted garlands of pink roses around the walls. There is a wooden dresser, a rocking chair, a brass bed, and a little table where I can write my poems. It was so quiet in my room that to stop the silence I opened my window. I could hear the leaves of the big poplar tree rattling and rustling just outside my window. So I knew I wasn't alone.

I hadn't thought much about trees before I came to Greenbush. They just seemed to be there like lampposts and buildings. Here in the country, where there aren't any buildings or lampposts, the trees stand out.

Early in the morning when I wake up, I can look out of the window and see Grandpapa walking in the orchard. He pays each tree a visit. He knows all of the fruit trees as well as he knows Grandmama and me.

There are other trees, too. When my mother was a girl, she planted a little maple tree. Now the tree reaches to the roof of the cottage. In front of the cottage are two weeping mulberry trees. Their branches hang all the way down to the ground. You can push the branches apart like a curtain and hide yourself in the little room the weeping branches make.

My favorite tree is an old apple tree. It teeters on the edge of the bank that leads down to the lake. Grandpapa says the apples are sour and wormy, and the tree isn't worth caring for. I like the tree because it makes an umbrella of shade where I can sit and read and keep an eye on the lake.

The Library

Alone,
walking slowly,
my city girl's bare feet
shy of glass and stone,
fields orange with hawkweed—
by whose hands
so many?

One look takes in the town,
awnings cranked down
against the sun
making pools of shade
cool to cross.

The library building
its age in stone 1859.
Floor, tables, chairs,
all oak

all with shiny skin
of varnish.
Sun stopped by
window shades
the color of dried moss.

Books leap
to my hands
green, tan, brown,
dog-eared.
I choose three,
their small weight
friendly
in my arms.

And home
I walk
three friends
with me now.

Everything is up! My garden has five green rows. Only what I had to do was awful. Grandmama said there were too many seedlings. ("Seedlings" is one of my favorite words now.) They were crowding each other out. So I had to pull some of them up and throw them away. I hated that.

Something else. I can walk barefoot. It took me a week to get used to going without shoes. When you're barefoot you can feel the softness of the dirt and the graininess of the sand and the sun's heat on the sidewalks in town. It's as if you're attached to the earth.

I walked to the library today because all the books I brought with me to read are used up. Though she had never set eyes on me before, the librarian, Miss Walther, greeted me with the kind of smile that says, "I knew you'd be coming." She was sitting at her desk with her glasses clamped to her nose and her white hair done up in a big puff with a pencil through it. When I said I would please like a library card, she wrote down my name without asking what it was.

I love the way libraries smell. If you just smell one book, it doesn't smell like that, but when you get a whole lot of books together in one room it's a papery, leathery, inky smell. The older the books, the better the smell. In the Greenbush library the books are so old that some of them have rubber bands around them to keep in the pages. In the back of the books, where people have signed them out, the handwriting is spidery and faded. Their names are different than ours. Girls were called Abigail and Sophia and Matilda. Boys were called Theodore and Amos and Joshua. I love the sound of the names and say them over to myself.

The library in Greenbush is different from the library in the city. In the city you know you couldn't read all the books in a million years. In Greenbush if you lived in the town all the time you would be able to read up one shelf and down the next. You could finish all the books in the library in a couple of years.

I took out *Eight Cousins* because I had only read it three times and *The Princess and the Goblin* because I had forgotten some parts in it and *Little Women* because I always take that out. When I got the books home, Grandpapa picked up each book and turned it over in his hand. "Yah, that's a good one," he said, although I was sure he had no idea what the book was about.

Grandmama just shook her head. "Sit and read all day and nothing gets done. A waste of time." But she gave me some cookies to eat under the apple tree.

I had just opened my book when out of the corner of my eye I caught a quick movement. It was a chipmunk. It crept close and sat up staring at me. I tossed it a piece of cookie. That scared it away, but in a minute it was back eating the crumb. I kept tossing the pieces closer and closer to me. The chipmunk crept up to me. He rested one paw on my hand while he nibbled the last piece of cookie. He was so busy eating he let me run a finger down his back. The fur was soft and warm. The bones were so delicate I was almost afraid to touch him. I stopped thinking all wild animals were ferocious.

The Rat

High
above the altar
of the country church,
God shines in the window
disguised as a dazzle of sun.
On this rainy Sunday
the window is dark.
A lie has crept
into my life
like a
long-
tailed
rat
and
nibbled
away
the
shimmer.

I wanted to go home. Back to the city. I missed my mother and father. I missed my aunts and uncles. I'd rather play with Lucille Macken than with a chipmunk. So one day while my grandparents were out weeding the vegetable garden I sneaked a sheet of paper and an envelope. I wrote a letter to my parents.

> Dear Mom and Dad,
> I hate it here. It's all vegetables and fruit and my grandparents are too old and there's no one for me to play with and there aren't enough books in the library and the lake won't go away. Come and get me before I die of boredom.
> Your loving daughter,
> Elsa

Here's the worst thing. I had spent all the money my mother had given me, and I didn't want to ask my grandparents for money. I would have had to explain why I wanted it, and I didn't want to hurt their feelings. So I stole a nickel from Grandmama's purse for a stamp. When I walked into town to mail the letter I felt like a policeman was following me. I told myself that no one would ever know, but I didn't believe me.

On Sunday, as they always do, my grandparents got all dressed up for church. Grandpapa lifted away the long board that kept the garage door shut. He backed out his old Packard. He drove us very slowly the three blocks to the Lutheran church. We could have walked faster than Grandpapa drove. His hands were so tight on the wheel and he was staring so hard at the road that you would have thought we were going a hundred miles an hour.

I sat next to Grandpapa. Grandmama sat in the back seat, very straight, with her head held up like a queen. She even waved at some people on the street as though they were her subjects. My grandparents are very proud of their car. It's ancient, but it looks new because it gets dusted every day and it's hardly ever driven. So when, halfway to church, it started raining, Grandpapa was upset. I'm sure he thought it would be much better for us to get wet walking than for the car to get wet.

Sitting in church, I could see the lightning and hear the thunder. I was really frightened. Pastor Auch's sermon was about Moses coming down from the mountain with the Ten Commandments. The pastor read every one of them. When he came to "Thou shalt not steal," there was a horrible clap of thunder. I wished I hadn't stolen the nickel. But worse was yet to come.

As we were leaving the church, Grandmama asked Pastor Auch if he and Mrs. Auch would like to come for Sunday dinner. I had never been in the same house with a minister, and I was sure that before the day was over he would discover what I had done. I guess I thought he had X-ray eyes and would be able to look right through me.

As soon as we got back to the cottage, Grandmama flew into the kitchen. In a minute's time the oven was stuffed, and all four burners on the stove were covered with pots. Grandpapa, with an apron tied around his waist, was peeling potatoes. I set the table with the good Haviland china and the cut-glass pickle dish.

I guess I expected Pastor Auch to come stamping into the house with his black suit, maybe shaking his fist. In the pulpit with his arms raised and his voice booming out, the pastor looked like a giant. The man who appeared at the front door of the cottage was short, with a plump belly and a big smile. Mrs. Auch was tiny and sort of hopped into the house like a sparrow.

There wasn't much time to worry about Pastor Auch finding out about what I had done, because right away the food started coming. There was chicken soup with home-made noodles; Koenigsberger Klopses, which are a sort of meatballs; mashed potatoes and gravy; string beans; sweet-sour lettuce with sugar and bacon and vinegar; biscuits; strawberry jam; and lemon meringue pie. Whenever anyone stopped talking for a minute, Grandmama would say, "Have another helping."

It was about halfway through dinner when Pastor Auch gave me a funny look and said, "I know a little secret about you." My heart was beating so hard I was sure everyone could hear it. I knew God had seen me steal the nickel, and I thought he had passed the word on to Pastor Auch. Pastor Auch leaned across the table. He fixed his eyes on me and said, "Your grandfather tells me you write poems."

I swallowed hard. "Yes, sir."

"I write poems, too," he said and gave me a sly wink.

"About baseball."

I guess my mouth dropped open because he explained, "Baseball is like life. We have our chances at bat and we have our innings. Sometimes we strike out and sometimes we hit a home run." He looked around the table to be sure everyone was impressed.

"You are so right, dear," Mrs. Auch said. Grandmama hurried to agree with her.

"Yah, yah," Grandpapa said, but he was holding his napkin to his mouth, and I could see he was trying not to laugh.

I breathed a sigh of relief, but I still knew that what I had done was wrong. Even when Mom's letter arrived saying, "We'll drive up next Sunday," I felt nothing good would come of it.

The only good thing today was that the rain made the lettuce in my garden grow a couple of inches. "In another week," Grandmama said, "we can have some of it for dinner."

"But it's so much smaller than the lettuce in your garden," I said.

"Yah," she said, putting an arm around me, "but little is more tender."

Broken Promises

The wild iris I gathered,
flights of purple birds
that withered overnight.
The mourning dove's nest
in the Scotch pine,
a cradle for two eggs,
two white promises,
until the red squirrel came
and left behind
a wreath of twigs.

All day I hear the sad cry of the mourning doves. I love the sound of their name when I say it aloud. They are big plump birds that like to perch on wires strung between the electric poles. They sit up there and cry their hearts out. Since I was feeling pretty sad myself, I liked to hear them. Grandmama says misery loves company.

I noticed one of the birds disappearing into the branches of a pine tree. After watching it fly back and forth from the tree several times, I crept quietly up to see what was there. Near the bottom of the tree was a ragged nest of twigs. I caught my breath. In the nest were two little white eggs. I hurried away as fast as I could.

After that I checked the nest each day. I never stayed more than a few seconds because I didn't want to scare off the mother bird.

Today was the day before my parents promised to come. I was feeling happier because I was sure they would take me home with them. I went to check the nest. I hoped the birds had hatched so I would have a chance to see them before I left.

It was still early morning, but already the sun was that white shimmering color it gets when it's going to be a hot day. In the field the grasshoppers bounced up and down ahead of me. I didn't see the mother dove, but I wasn't worried. Sometimes she was gone from the nest for several minutes. As I got closer to the tree, a red squirrel scurried out of a branch near the nest and began chattering crossly at me.

The red squirrels were my favorite squirrels. Compared to the big bushy-tailed ones, the tiny red squirrels with the white bellies and fur-tufted ears were like toys. Grandpapa didn't like them. "Those red squirrels," he said, "they're little but they do a lot of mischief." I thought he was talk-

41

ing about his fruit trees.

The squirrel leaped to a higher branch and then jumped to a nearby tree. I looked down into the nest. Instead of the two eggs I expected to see, there were broken bits of white shell. I knew the red squirrel had eaten the eggs.

I ran crying to Grandmama, who tried to comfort me. "The birds will build another nest," she said. "The red squirrel doesn't know any better. He was only looking for food. Think of all the eggs we eat." I made a vow never to eat another egg.

"Come. I'll show you something," Grandmama said. I followed her into the living room. "Look there at the rug. No fringe." It was true. The fringe on the long red-and-white-striped rag rug had disappeared. She tiptoed across the room to the bookshelf and pulled out a handful of books. Behind the books was a nest made out of shreds that once had been the fringe on the rug. Inside the nest were five naked baby mice scrunched into a pink squirming ball. She put the books back. "Never mind the mourning doves," she said. "You can keep an eye on the mice." I felt like I had been given something back.

Later I heard Grandpapa say, "But Gussie, you told me to get rid of the mice. You had a conniption when you found the nest. I never thought I'd live to see the day you allowed mice to run around in our house."

"Well, Carl, I've changed my mind. Leave them be. We'll have mice instead of doves."

"What do you mean? Since when has there been a dove in the living room?"

Grandmama just laughed.

There was another disaster. This one in my garden. The lettuce was all chomped up by some rabbits. But it was easier to forgive the rabbits than the red squirrel. The lettuce would come up again.

In the afternoon when I went into town to get the mail, the postmistress handed me a letter from my parents. It said they wouldn't be coming after all. "There is something wrong with our car," Mom wrote. "I'm afraid it will be a few weeks before there is money to fix it. Your father still hasn't found a job. I know you will understand." She said it was hot in the city. I was lucky to be near the lake. She was sure that by now I was getting to like the country. She sent her love.

This time I couldn't cry because I was in town where people could see me. Right across the street squinting at me was the boy with the red hair. I would have died before I let him see me cry. I couldn't even run home to Grandmama for comfort. I couldn't tell her I had written my parents to come and take me home.

When I got back to the cottage, Grandmama must have seen that something was wrong because she said to me, "With a face like that you could curdle milk." Then she rolled up her sleeves and made strawberry shortcake, which she knew was my favorite dessert.

The Gully

When they call my name
I run away to a hidden place.
Down the bank I hand myself
from tree to tree toward
the dark trickle of creek,
the boggy tangle of snarled
willows and grasses where frogs
squat like slippery green stones
and swallowtails and dragon flies
sit on my knees.

I can't believe I made myself climb down into the gully
today. The sides of the gully are steep. To keep from
falling I had to grab at bushes and tree trunks. When I
finally got to the bottom, I was surprised to find a little

creek. All this time I hadn't known the creek was hidden down there. The grassy banks on either side of the creek stick up like the walls of a green room. Overhead the sky is a blue ceiling. My room is furnished with fallen trees for chairs and boulders for tables. There are jewel weed and wild iris for decoration.

I'm not the only one who uses the room. Birds are everywhere. There are large black birds at the top of the trees and bluebirds and red birds. There are birds that hammer so hard on the trees you would think their brains would get rattled. There are small yellow birds that fly around together. When I sit quietly the birds splash in the creek and snatch at the flies that hover over the water. Once a yellow and black butterfly landed on me. I knew what it was because my grandfather said butterflies like that are called swallowtails. I liked the word so much that I kept it.

I sit on a log and watched the trickle of water move over the bright stones and sandy ridges of the creek bottom. There are bugs that walk on the water. The creek moves so quickly that I thought it must be anxious to get someplace. I decided to see where it was going.

The floor of the gully is squishy to walk on. Frogs jump out at you. In some places the grass is as tall as I am. When you're exploring, the best thing is that you don't know what's coming next. That's the most frightening thing, too.

I kept on walking in the direction the water was going. After a bit I saw a clearing ahead. There was the beach, and beyond it the lake!

Standing in the lake was Grandmama. She had her skirts tucked up to her knees. She was bending over, washing her hair. I had never seen her hair undone. It spread out on the water in brown swirls. After squeezing out the water, she sat down on a large rock at the water's edge to dry her hair in the sun. With her hair around her shoulders and her face turned to the sun, she looked as young as my mother. There was a smile on her face, and I saw that Grandmama has thoughts that have nothing to do with me or Grandpapa. She has secret thoughts just like I do. That was as much a surprise to me as finding the creek hidden in the gully.

Air Mail

*The ocean is wider
than the lake,
across its distance
their letter
calls our name.
With pen and ink
we pull them toward us.
We write,
"Hurry."*

I went to the library today to take books out about birds
and flowers. I want to keep track of everything I see in
the gully. After I went to the library I stopped at the post
office. There was a letter for my grandparents. It was
written on thin white paper with a lot of strange stamps.

Letters like that come from Europe.

When I gave it to Grandpapa he said to Grandmama, "It's from Kurt Roth." As he opened the letter, his hands shook so that he tore a bit of it. "They have closed his art gallery and taken away all of the paintings." Grandpapa's face was pale. "What harm could they see in paintings of flowers and trees and sailboats?"

"Kurt always had his own way of painting things. That's what they don't like. Does he say how Ruth is?"

"She has been dismissed from her position with the school. It is becoming too dangerous for them to stay in Berlin. He says many artists have already left. Kurt says there may be a way for him to get out of Germany. He wants to know if we could find him work here."

"Why do they have to leave Germany?" I asked.

My grandparents had forgotten that I was there. Now they gave me a long look.

"She's too young to hear such things," Grandpapa said.

"She has already heard them," Grandmama answered.

Grandpapa sighed. "It is a terrible thing, Elsa, but because our friends, Kurt and Ruth, are Jewish, the German government has taken away their living. Hitler is telling artists what they must paint and writers what they must write. Now it is not even safe for Jews to be seen on the streets. It is hard to remember when we are so comfortable here that people can be so very cruel. Our friends will have to give up their home and everything they own and come away."

"If they are lucky enough to escape," Grandmama said. "Write them at once, Carl. We must do all we can to help them."

Grandpapa sat down at the kitchen table to write his reply. "As soon as I finish, Elsa, you can take my letter into Greenbush and mail it."

While he wrote, Grandmama bustled about making noodles, folding the dough and chopping it into long strands. Whenever she is upset she cooks something, usually something that takes a lot of pounding or chopping.

When the letter was finished, I took it to the post office. Grandmama had given me some paper to carry it in so I wouldn't get fingerprints on the envelope or smudge the writing. I studied the address as I dropped it into the mail slot. I had looked up Germany once on the map, and I knew how far away it was. I wondered if the letter would get there in time.

Talk

*All week long
my grandparents
explain themselves,
their talk scrambling
my thoughts.*

*Tonight I am greedy
for my own company,
hungry to know
what I am up to.*

*When I sit in a room
listening to people
a branch taps at the window
and the tree outside is me.*

Every night after supper is over I settle into one of the big overstuffed chairs in the living room to listen to my grandparents. They talk about how the corn and beans and peas and tomatoes are coming along. They talk about the apple and plum and peach and pear trees. In detail. It is almost as though they are talking the garden and orchard into growing. It seems like all their words will turn into carrots and apples and beans.

They tell me stories about what it was like in Germany. "Christmas was the best," Grandmama said. "Relatives and friends filled our house. The *Tannenbaum* reached to the ceiling and was lit by little candles. It was decorated with gingerbread and marzipan."

"What is marzipan?" I asked, already deciding to keep the words *"Tannenbaum"* and "marzipan."

"Candies made from almond paste molded into wonderful shapes. They are wrapped in gold and silver tinfoil."

Grandpapa told me about the museums full of great paintings and the concerts and opera. They were all on a beautiful street in the city of Berlin called *Unter den Linden*, which means "beneath the linden trees."

Some of the stories I had heard before. My grandparents are getting old. I think they want to tell me the stories so that the stories will stay in my head. They hope one day I'll tell them to someone else and the stories will always be remembered.

After a while I got tired of all the talk. I could hear the crickets outside and the rustle of the trees creaking in the wind. My mind flew out the window where no one could get to it. Grandpapa must have seen how restless I was, because the next morning he said, "We have a surprise for you. Tonight they are showing a movie in the town, and I bought you a ticket."

"But there's no movie house," I said, suddenly homesick for Detroit's big theaters that are like palaces—all gold with statues and heavy velvet curtains that drag silk fringe.

"They put up a tent on the fairgrounds," Grandmama explained. "You must remember to take a pillow. The seats are hard."

"And a flashlight," Grandpapa added, "for the trip home."

It was a strange way to go to the movies, I thought, carrying a pillow and a flashlight.

"What are they showing, Carl?" Grandmama asked.

"The girl who sold the tickets didn't know. A western, perhaps."

I felt important walking into town all by myself when it was almost dark out. I didn't want to be seen carrying the pillow, so I hid it behind a tree where I could get it on the way back. Grandmama had made me wear shoes, and I hid those, too. In some of the houses along the street the lights had already been turned on. People were sitting around their tables having a late dinner or were gathered around the radio. Being able to look into the lighted windows was almost as good as watching a movie.

At one of the houses a man and a woman were rocking

back and forth on a porch swing, watching their children playing in the front yard. I thought of my mom and dad at home and my friends who were probably out playing games. They were probably having fun and not even thinking of me. I must have been staring because the children stopped to watch me pass by. If they had asked me to play with them I would have forgotten all about the movie.

When I got to the fairgrounds I saw a huge tent. I joined the people who were crowding into the entrance to find seats on the benches. Hundreds of moths were gathered around the lantern that hung from the ceiling of the tent. In the back of the tent was the motion-picture projector with two thick reels of film. The lantern went out, and the name of the film flashed on the screen. It wasn't a western. It was *Dracula!* There was a lot of applause and whistles and screeches. A couple of parents with young children got up and left in a huff.

Glaring out at us from the screen was Dracula, with a horrible face and teeth like a wolf. There wasn't any sound, just words printed on the screen to let you know what the characters were saying. Something told me I should leave, too. I was sure my grandparents had no idea of what I was seeing. But there was Dracula wrapping himself in his cape and smiling at a lady with long curls, too much lipstick, and a long, white, naked throat. I stayed. I don't know which was the worst part. It was either the blood dripping from Dracula's long teeth or those thuds as they pounded the stake through Dracula's heart. When the picture was over, I was so frightened I couldn't move. The redheaded pest I had seen in town was sitting behind me. "You better get out," he hissed, "or you and Dracula will be the only ones left." I gave him a furious look, but I hurried out.

For a couple of blocks it was all right. There were lots of people walking home, and I just stayed with them. By the time I got farther out of town, most of the people were gone. Soon I was the only one. I walked as fast as I could and kept shining my flashlight all around me. In the dark, the familiar road home had disappeared. In the daytime trees lean over you in a friendly way. At night they seem to be reaching out to grab you. I was running so fast that I had a pain in my side. Moths attracted by my flashlight fluttered around me.

Then the second-worst thing happened. A fluttering shape swooped at me. It was a bat. I guess it was after the moths that were flying around my flashlight, but it seemed to be coming right at me. I dropped the flashlight and clutched my throat. It could have been Dracula turned into a bat. The dark shape flew off, and I groped around for the flashlight. Something had happened to it when it fell, and it wouldn't go on.

I kept on running. Then the worst thing happened. I stepped on something lumpy. It was soft, and it moved! I jumped a mile, and whatever it was—a toad or a frog—got out of there. After that, all I remember was racing down the path to the cottage and throwing myself inside the door. "Elsa!" Grandmama said. "What has happened?"

She put her arms around me and patted my back. I hung on as tightly as I could. After a while I let go and told them about Dracula.

"It was my fault," Grandpapa said. "I should have found out what the movie was."

No one asked me where the pillow was or where my shoes were. I'd get them in the morning. And I decided that the next night I'd stay home and listen to my grandparents' stories.

The Great Lake

Its jeweler's window
offers bright stones,
wheedles me with shells.
Its little waves
lick me like a dog,
sing me to sleep.
But the selfish lake
never lets me
see the secret
of its other shore.

The last thing I hear at night before I fall asleep is the sound of the waves slapping against the shore. The first thing I see in the morning is the reflection on my ceiling of sun glittering on the water.

For a long time I was afraid of the lake, but I loved its wide, sandy beach. I'd climb down the stairway to the beach, past the pump house where the water from the lake is pumped up to our cottage, and past the poison ivy. When I first came, Grandpapa showed me the three green leaves you have to watch out for. I forgot all about it, and one evening there were itchy blisters all up and down my legs. Grandmama mixed up baking soda and water and put it on the blisters. After that I was careful to watch where I walked.

You can sit on the beach where the sand is dry and start digging. When the hole in the sand gets deep enough, water creeps into the hole. It's as if the lake is hiding, just waiting for you to find it.

You can walk for miles along the beach. Every few feet you find something to keep. The top of my dresser was heaped with things leaking sand: snail shells to turn into bracelets, gulls' feathers, tangles of driftwood. My favorite finds are the pieces of glass that have been in the lake for years and years. The water and the sand have rubbed all the sharp edges smooth.

I'd see a pretty stone or shell in the lake and reach for it. When a wave chased me, I'd jump back. It was as if someone were offering you a piece of candy and when you put your hand out for it they snatched it away.

Finally I made myself stand there and let the waves wash over my legs and splash my bathing suit. Little by little the lake invited me into it. I got so that I laughed at the waves, diving into them and letting them carry me back to shore. I floated facedown, my eyes open. I watched bubbles gurgle up from clam shells and snails inch along the slippery stones. Minnows came and nibbled at my toes.

I know there will be days when I am still afraid of the lake. Days when the storms come. Days when the waves leap and foam, striking the beach and rushing out again to become more and bigger waves. Days when the fishing boats head for the pier. On those days I'll hurry inside. Then the lake, like a spoiled child, will have everything for itself.

Meyer's Fish House

The
Billy
Boy *in and*
the fish hand-
clapping their
tails against the
bottom of the boat;
Mr. Meyer in overalls,
the knife in his hand.
The pearl scales fly,
the little dead pearl
of the eye, the fish
mouth curved in the
sleepy child smile,
scraps floating
on the water
like a dainty
treat, and all the gulls
that came flying to the party.

The main street of Greenbush ends at a pier, a long dock that sticks out into the lake. Early in the morning the fishing boats set out from the pier. Late in the afternoon they come back, their decks heaped with whitefish and perch and pickerel. If the wind blows toward the town you can smell the fish long before you get to the pier.

Yesterday Grandmama sent me to Mr. Meyer's Fish House to buy perch for supper. I got there early because I like to watch the boats come in. The first boat in was the *Billy Boy*. It's owned by Billy Harper, who is so tall and so fat there is hardly room for anyone else on his boat. His brother goes out with him, and sometimes his son goes out, too. His son is my age. He's the redheaded pest.

As Mr. Harper was tying up his boat, he called to the other fishermen to ask how many fish each boat had caught. The fishermen like to brag about how large their catch is, but they are careful to keep secret where they spread their nets.

Mr. Harper and his brother carried boxes full of fish, most of them still alive, into the fish house. Mr. Harper's son just stood on the boat looking at me. I thought if I didn't say something his eyes would pop out. "Hello," I said. "What's your name?"

"Tommy. What's yours?"

"Elsa. Do you help your dad?"

"Sure. I help let out the nets and then I help take them in. You want to see my calluses?" He held out his hands, and I could see where the skin was hardened. "I was out in a storm once with my dad and he had to tie me onto the boat so I wouldn't fall over and drown. I can't swim."

"If you're out on the lake all the time, why doesn't your dad or your uncle teach you to swim?"

"They can't swim either."

I thought that was really dumb. Off the top of my head I said, "I'll teach you to swim and then you can teach your father and uncle."

"I don't think so. I don't like the water."

"But you're out on it all the time. Aren't you going to be a fisherman like your dad?"

"Sure."

I told him where I lived. "Do you work on Sunday?"

He shook his head. Besides his red hair he has a face full of freckles, and his watery blue eyes blink a lot. He's tall and scrawny, not fat like his dad.

"Well then, come on over to our beach around three o'clock." I left him to go into the fish house. The fish house is a big building where the fish are cleaned and scaled. Mr. Meyer wears a long rubber apron. He has glasses that keep getting scales on them.

"Heads on or off?" he asked me.

"On." Grandmama says the heads give the fish more flavor.

He wrapped the perch up in thick white paper and tied the package with string. By the time I got home, my hands smelled of fish. Grandmama rubbed my hands with lemon to take away the smell. I think they must use a lot of lemons at Mr. Meyer's house.

On Sunday afternoon I waited for Tommy on the

beach. He came trudging up the beach about an hour late. "You didn't bring your bathing suit," I said.

"Don't have one. I don't care if I get my shorts wet."

"Come out where the water is deeper." I began to wade into the lake. Tommy stayed on the shore. I knew how he felt. I used to feel the same way, but I worried that if he didn't learn to swim he might drown someday. "Come on," I coaxed. He didn't move. "Just up to your ankles." He shook his head. Suddenly I started running at him, splashing the cold water onto him as hard as I could.

He yelped and plunged into the water to chase me. I ran out deeper and deeper, calling him names. Soon we were both up to our necks. He suddenly realized where he was and began to squeal. I lay on my back and kicked my feet. "Let your feet go up," I said. He watched me kick my way toward the shore, and then he did the same thing. He was kicking like crazy. I showed him how to float and how to do the sidestroke. He learned fast, but each time he couldn't wait to get out of the water.

Later, when we were lying on the sand drying off, Tommy asked me, "Who taught you to swim?"

"My dad taught me in the city. There's a park called Belle Isle near our apartment."

"I'd rather die than live in the city. The city is full of gangsters."

"It is not," I said. "I've lived in the city all my life, and I've never seen a gangster."

"You probably just don't know one when you see one. Your grandparents are Krauts, aren't they?"

"Krauts isn't a nice word. They came from Germany, but they're Americans now."

"That's what *they* say. If we have a war with Germany they'll be on Germany's side, and they'll have to go to prison."

I thought about how the people had stoned Grandpapa's car when he was on the way to the hospital because he was German. I thought about the Roths and how some of the Germans hated them because they were Jewish. I hated Tommy for saying such mean things. "I'm sorry I taught you to swim," I screamed at him. "I hope you drown!" I ran up the steps to our cottage. Halfway up the stairs I bumped into Grandpapa on his way down to the pump house.

"What's all this shouting?" He held on to me. "Where are you running to? Who is that boy?"

"He's horrible. He called you a Kraut and said they'd put you in jail."

"*Ach*, Elsa. Go and wash your face and tell your grandmother to put out a plate of cookies and some raspberry juice."

A few minutes later Grandpapa appeared with Tommy. He brought him into the kitchen, where Grandmama had set the table. He said to her, "This young man needs a little something for his stomach. Pass him some cookies, Elsa."

I shoved the plate of cookies at Tommy, but I wouldn't look at him. Grandmama poured him a big glass of juice. He wolfed down about five cookies and drank two glasses of raspberry juice. "Those cookies are good," he said. The whole time he was eating he kept looking around the cottage as if he expected German spies to poke their heads out of closets.

"Doesn't your mother make you cookies, Tommy?" Grandmama asked.

"My mom took off. It's just Dad and me, and he don't cook. Even if he did, we don't have a lot of food like here."

"Well, at least you must have plenty of fish for dinner," Grandpapa said.

"I hate fish. It's about all we got to eat. When do you have supper?" he asked.

"Another hour or two," Grandmama said. "We would be happy to have you stay."

"Thanks," Tommy grinned.

"Go and show Tommy the orchard and your garden, Elsa," Grandpapa said.

I headed for the front yard, not even looking to see if Tommy was following me. I didn't understand why my grandparents were so polite to Tommy when he said such awful things about them. If they wanted to kill him with kindness, I wished the killing would come first and the kindness later.

Tommy was tagging along behind me. When we got outside he said, "I'm sorry I called them Krauts. They're OK."

Out in the orchard I said, "I'll bet I can climb up this tree before you can climb up that one." He started shinnying up the tree I pointed to. Unfortunately, he saw the hornets' nest before the hornets could get him, so he didn't get stung. And he ate like a pig at supper. And he promised to come back.

Chickens

I liked visiting the chicken farm.
I liked watching chickens
in their white ruffled dresses,
yellow kneesocks,
red hair bows,
gabbling like schoolgirls
fenced in at recess time,
until one day we found
the farmer's wife,
a pot of scalding water
between her knees,
her hands full of feathers,
grinning, "You'll never
get a fresher one than this."

On Sundays we have chicken for dinner. Grandmama's chicken is always perfect: goldenbrown on the outside and tender on the inside. Every Saturday we go to the Tolkens's farm to buy the chicken. We buy butter and eggs there, too, and thick whipping cream. My grandmama calls the cream *schlag* and heaps it on all our desserts.

Mrs. Tolken keeps the butter and cream in the spring house, which is just a stone shed over a little stream. The stream comes up from the ground. It is so cold that everything in the shed is chilled even on the hottest day. While my grandparents talk with Mrs. Tolken, I wander around the farm. I watch the chickens take dust baths, which seems like a strange kind of bath. I listen to them talking to one another. "Gabbling," Mrs. Tolken calls it, a good word to keep. In the barn there are two horses, Andy and Ben. I feed them lumps of sugar I've sneaked. In back of the barn is the sty. I always go there to see if the pigs have any new piglets.

Of course I *knew* it was a chicken we were buying from the Tolkens, but I never connected the newspaper-wrapped package we carried home with the chickens that I loved to watch running around in the yard. Then one day we got to the farm a little early. Mrs. Tolken called to us from her back porch. "Just about to pluck your chicken," she said. "I'm a little behind myself today."

She had one of the beautiful feathery white chickens by the throat. It was dead. She dipped the dead chicken into a pail of scalding water. Then she pulled at its feathers. They came out in her hands like the petals off of a flower. The scrawny chicken was left naked. Its skin looked like it had goose bumps.

On the way back to our car I wouldn't look at the live chickens running around. I promised myself I'd never eat another chicken as long as I lived.

The next day Grandmama baked the chicken as usual. Every time Grandmama opened the oven to baste the chicken it gave off a heavenly smell. But I told myself I wouldn't touch it. We were just going to sit down at the table when we heard a car in the driveway. It was my Aunt Fritzie and Uncle Tim.

Even if there isn't any money for her clothes, Aunt Fritzie always wears something fashionable. She can cut up old clothes, or dishtowels, or slipcovers and turn them into a wonderful outfit. That day she wore something pale blue and gauzy that Grandmama recognized right away. "Fritzie, those are your living-room curtains!"

"It's much more stylish these days to have bare windows," Aunt Fritzie said. She put her arms around me, and I could smell the perfume she always wore. "Well, Elsa, don't you look terrific. We went to see the movie *Little Women* last week, and I said to your Uncle Tim, 'Amy looks just like Elsa.' " The thing about Aunt Fritzie is that she always makes you feel good, even if you know the nice things she says aren't the truth.

She is artistic, too. She cuts out pictures of sleeping babies from magazines. She pastes them on tiny silk cushions and dresses them in handembroidered bonnets and little shawls trimmed with bits of lace. When the pictures are finished, she frames them and sells them.

Uncle Tim is Irish. He is handsome, with slick black hair and a black mustache. Before the Depression, they had money, and Aunt Fritzie loved to dress him up just like she dressed up the pictures of the babies. She bought him silk shirts and golf knickers and black-and-white shoes. One Christmas she gave him blue satin pajamas and matching blue satin sheets. But the satin sheets and pajamas were so slippery that each time Uncle Tim turned over he slid out of bed. Even now, when he had been out of work for months, he was wearing a straw hat and a white suit that looked new.

They acted surprised that we were just sitting down to dinner, but they ate an awful lot. There was plenty, though, because Grandmama always cooks extra. During dinner Uncle Tim did tricks, like pulling out a napkin from under a glass of water without spilling any water, which made Grandmama nervous.

After dinner Uncle Tim played records on the Victrola. He has a fine tenor voice, and he sang along and got us to sing, too, even Grandmama. Before they left, Aunt Fritzie asked me to show her all the things I had collected from the beach. She took a long time looking at them, and she said when she was my age she collected all the same things. As we came downstairs I heard Grandpapa say in an angry voice, "You spend money on a new suit, but you want to borrow money for groceries."

Uncle Tim said, "If I want to get a job I have to look

prosperous. No one will hire a salesman who looks like he's down on his luck."

Grandpapa sighed and took out his wallet. There wasn't much in it. Grandmama got up and went into the pantry. In a few minutes she was back with more money. Aunt Fritzie threw her arms around Grandmama and Grandpapa and cried a little. But soon she was laughing and Uncle Tim was making jokes and they were in their car waving cheerfully to us as they drove away.

"Will they ever learn, Carl?" Grandmama said.

"They have a way of forgetting unhappy things," Grandpapa said. "Maybe that's not so bad."

It was only then that I realized I had forgotten all about Mrs. Tolken. I had eaten the chicken. Two helpings!

Grandfather

He paints pictures
with blood-red roses,
their petals
thick as meat,
orange lilies,
open-mouthed
and yawning,
pink peonies
fat as pigs.
When he finishes
a painting,
he walks
around the garden,
grumbling
at how dull
real flowers are.

I like to watch Grandpapa paint. His painting clothes have little smears and dabs of paint on the pants and shirt. You can match the colors of the spots with the pictures he has painted.

On the porch he sets up his easel to hold his painting. He squeezes a little paint from nearly every tube onto his palette. When the colors are all arranged, he opens a book that has pictures of flowers in it. First he draws the flowers from the book, then he paints them. In the book the flowers never look real. They never look real in Grandpapa's pictures either. The pink flowers are too pink and the blue flowers too blue. And everything is too large.

With the yard full of flowers, I don't know why my grandpapa paints flowers out of a book. This morning I asked, "Grandpapa, why don't you pick some of the flowers in the garden and paint them?"

"*Ach*," he said, "they're nothing special. I can't do anything with them."

Grandmama, who had been listening, laughed. "You mean you can't make them do what you want them to do."

"In Berlin," Grandpapa said, "my teacher said you must learn to paint by studying the paintings of famous painters. I used to go into the Old Museum with my easel and paints to copy the pictures. That museum had twenty paintings by the great artist Rembrandt. Imagine!"

"Ah, but just down the street was the Café Bauer," Grandmama said. "We would have cups of chocolate. From a table covered with silver trays we would pick out cookies shaped like swans. *Hohlhippen*, we called them. They were made with the beaten whites of eggs and were so light you didn't know you held them in your hand. And all the while you sipped your chocolate a string quartet played waltzes."

Grandpapa frowned. "Gussie," he said, "how can you compare the beauty of a great painting by Rembrandt with a cookie?"

"You can live without pictures, Carl, but even an artist has to eat." Grandmama went into the kitchen and brought back a big plate of sugar cookies.

"You win, Gussie," Grandpapa said. We ate up all the cookies.

Later Grandpapa said to me, "Elsa, you mustn't be like me when you write your poems. You mustn't just copy what other people have done. Everyone has their own painting and their own poem inside them. Everyone has something they can say that no one else can say for them."

When I went up to my room I looked through my diary. What my grandfather said is true. No one else could have written exactly what I wrote, and if I didn't write it, it would never get said.

The Dummy

Because I kept
to myself,
reading
my books,
she made a dummy,
stuffing newspaper
into one of my dresses,
twisting paper
into arms and legs,
rolling it into a ball
painted with eyes
and a mouth.
Open on its lap
lay a book.
Hung around the neck
was my name.

I sit under the leafy branches of the apple tree and read my books. There is nothing to bother me but birds hunting the caterpillars that fold themselves up in leaves.

From time to time Grandmama comes to see what I am doing. "You'll ruin your eyes," she says, or "Heavens, girl, why don't you *do* something?"

When I answer, "I am doing something, Grandmama. I'm reading," she sends me out to pick strawberries or weed my garden. After a few minutes she is there to tell me, "You're forgetting to look under the leaves. That's where the biggest berries are." Or, "Child, you're pulling up your flower seedlings instead of weeds!" She sighs and tells me to go back to my books. Soon she will be there with another chore.

"I don't think it's healthy that you should read so much." Grandmama picks up my book and leafs through it as if she were looking for some creepy-crawly thing inside.

One morning, on my way to the screen porch where we have our breakfasts, I saw it sitting in a rocking chair—a dummy made of newspapers stuffed into one of my dresses. There was a book on its lap. I started to cry. Grandpapa put his arm around me. "She only meant it as a joke," he said.

"But why is she so against my reading?" I asked.

"In the old country your grandmama loved to read. But when she came to this country, she was too shy or too proud to go to school to learn to read English like I did. She misses her books just as you would. You must never tell her I told you that. She doesn't like people to know."

I tried to think what it would mean not to be able to read. It would be like walking into the library and taking down books from the shelves only to find that they were all glued shut.

Later that morning when I was sitting under the apple tree, Grandmama came to tell me to pick up the rugs on the porch and shake the sand out of them. "Wait a minute, Grandmama," I said. "I've just come to a good part in my book. Let me finish it. I'll read it out loud so you can hear it, too."

She gave me a sharp look. "I've got better things to do with my time than to listen to books." But she sat down.

I was reading *Little Women*, so I knew just where to turn. I read her the part where Beth dies. I read how Beth grew too weak to sew anymore. How Beth found the sad poem her sister, Jo, wrote about her. How Beth died in her mother's arms with just a sigh.

"Well," Grandmama said, wiping away a tear, "Beth is with the angels."

Now two or three times a day Grandmama comes out to where I am reading and says, "Well, what is that wild girl, Jo, doing now?" She sits down under the tree with her long skirt arranged neatly and her legs in their thick white cotton stockings sticking straight out. I read to her. After a while she gets up and shakes the grass from her skirt. "I can't sit here all day wasting time," she says, but she always comes back. The dummy is gone.

The Card Game

In the orchard,
proper in suits
and Panama hats,
Willie Hoffman, Gustave
Ladamacher,
and my grandfather
are playing cards,
the smoke from their cigars
bothering butterflies,
their German insults
knocking apples
off the trees.

Every Saturday afternoon Mr. Ladamacher and another German gentleman come to play cards with Grandpapa. Every Saturday morning Grandmama makes strudel. Every week the German gentlemen act surprised, as if they had never seen strudel before. "*Himmel!*" they say. That means, "heaven." "Gussie made strudel for us! So much work just for us!"

Grandmama always replies, "*Ach*, there's nothing to it."

But there is a lot to the making of strudel. I love to watch how it's done. First Grandmama scoops out a big pile of flour and makes a hole in the center of it. Eggs and water and butter go into the hole. Using her hands, Grandmama squishes the mess together. Then it's pounded and kneaded. That's just the beginning. The dough sits for a while, "rests," Grandmama calls it, as if the dough were snoozing. She spreads a clean cloth over the kitchen table and sprinkles flour over it. Next she rolls out the dough and begins to pull it with the backs of her hands. Little by little, the lump of dough stretches and grows. I get to help with the stretching. When we're finished, the strudel dough, so thin you can see through it, covers the whole tabletop. By then Grandmama has flour all over her, even on the tip of her nose.

She spreads sliced apples and raisins and sugar and cinnamon over the strudel dough. She rolls it all up into a long bundle and bakes it. Nothing smells better than an oven full of strudel.

When the strudel is all finished, Grandmama puts it on her china platter with the roses painted all over it and lets me carry the strudel out into the orchard where the men are playing euchre. I'm not sure what kind of card game euchre is, but it seems like you can't play it without a lot of shouting and yelling. Since the shouting all goes on in German, the only word I understand is *dummkopf,* which means "dumbbell." I know that word. It is what my grandmama calls herself when a hole opens up in the strudel dough she is pulling and she has to patch it.

One day I climbed up into an apple tree near where the men were playing. After a while they must have forgotten I was there. They were full of strudel. Their Panama hats were tipped back from their foreheads, and their ties were loosened. Their jackets hung from the backs of their chairs, and their shirtsleeves were rolled up. Grandpapa was passing around a box of cigars. Grandpapa saves the rings around the cigars for me. He gives me the cigar boxes, too. I kept the baby mice in one of them. I don't think the mice liked the smell of the cigars, though, because they ran away.

The men looked over their shoulders toward the cottage. Grandmama was inside washing dishes. I saw Grandpapa take out of his jacket pocket what looked like a small bottle, only it was metal not glass. He held it under the table and carefully unscrewed the top. The bottle was passed around, and everyone took a quick sip from it. Hurriedly Grandpapa put the bottle back in his pocket. I heard them say the word *Schnaps.*

Later I asked Grandmama what *Schnaps* meant. "Where did you hear that word?" she wanted to know.

"In the orchard. They were drinking it from a little bottle."

"Ach! Sie haben Schnaps getrunken. Schnaps is whiskey. Your grandfather makes it himself."

"But isn't it against the law to make whiskey?" It was Prohibition, and no one was allowed to buy or sell whiskey.

"It's just in case someone gets sick. Then we take a little for medicine. Maybe Mr. Ladamacher ate too much strudel and needed a little of the medicine." She looked at me to see if I believed her. A minute later she was marching across the orchard toward the men. I could hear her scolding them in German all the way up to the cottage.

Quick Change

The city is an old woman
with nothing to dress up for,
the country, a young girl
trying on one thing and then another,
skirts of purple knotweed,
scarves of yellow mustard,
ribbons of red clover.

In the mornings after breakfast, Grandmama works in her garden pulling weeds. She ties up the leggy blue larkspur and waters the plants with a sprinkling can she fills from the rain barrel. The water in our faucets is pumped from the lake. "Too cold for the flowers," Grandmama says.

While she works in her garden, I work in mine. All the vegetables are up, and there are little beans starting. The snapdragons are blooming, too. I picked some to go on the dining room table. Grandmama helped me cage my tomato plants. They are growing so large they can't hold themselves up, so they go in these wire cages. First there were little yellow flowers all over the plants, and now there are tiny green tomatoes. "Why does it take so long for everything to grow?" I asked Grandmama.

She put her arm around me. It was warm from the sun, and she smelled of the tomato plants, which is a nice smell. "*Ach*, what is your hurry? Enjoy today. Tomorrow will come soon enough."

I think she was talking about me and not the tomatoes.

In the fields something amazing is happening. One week the fields are orange with hawkweed, another week gold with mustard. Then they are white with daisies. I think of how hard I have to work to make my small garden grow. These fields, with their thousands and thousands of flowers, stretch as far as your eye can see.

There are flowers that know enough to open their blossoms in the morning and close them at night, as if they were keeping store. There are plants that have special friends: the milkweed flowers are cluttered with fluttering orange butterflies called monarchs. The tall yellow mullein plant has a yellow goldfinch perched on its tip.

I go by the fields on my way into Greenbush to get the mail. No letter has come from the Roths. On the way home the fields are still crowded with flowers. Far away in

Germany, too, there are fields of flowers, but if you were my grandparents' friends the government might forbid you to paint the flowers. It would be like the flowers were taken away from you.

Each time I go into Greenbush I try to keep out of Tommy's way. Most of the time Tommy's on the fishing boat with his dad, but today he was sitting on the drugstore steps. When he's with the other kids he doesn't pay any attention to me. Today he was alone, so he said, "You want to see something?"

"What?" I wanted to know.

"In Mr. Hatton's workshop."

"I don't care." Just this morning Grandmama had mentioned a table she admired in Mr. Hatton's store.

I guess I should have been warned by the sneaky way Tommy prowled around to the back of the furniture store.

"Why can't we just go in the store?" I asked.

"Because what he's working on is special, and he doesn't want anyone to see it." Tommy climbed up on a wooden crate that was pushed against the back wall of the store. He peered into a window and then motioned to me to climb up next to him.

By standing on my toes and stretching my neck up I could just see into the room. Scattered around the room were hammers and saws and all the stuff carpenters have. In the middle of the room was a sort of table. A man was lying on it. He was very still. "Why is that man sleeping on a table?" I asked Tommy.

"He isn't sleeping. He's dead as a doornail. It's old Mr.

Spire. He croaked last night, and Mr. Hatton's building him his coffin."

I practically fell off the crate. It was worse than Dracula. "You brought me here to show me a dead man!"

"What's the matter with that?"

I didn't even bother to answer him. As far as I'm concerned, he can get in his fishing boat and go to China.

The Violin

Like a whirlwind
out spins a waltz
from the window
and winds me
against my will.

By the speckled light of fireflies,
feet slippery with dew,
I dance on the darkened lawn
to my grandfather's violin.

To make such music
you must break
yourself open like an egg,
and dazzled,
I dance on the shell.

If Grandmama is moody and sometimes angry, Grandpapa always seems to be the same. Each morning from my bedroom window I see him walking in the orchard. He is checking every tree to be sure it got through the night all right.

If something in the pictures he paints doesn't turn out right, he sighs and patiently paints it over.

When the pump that brings in our water from the lake breaks down, he isn't upset. He just goes into the pump house with his wrenches and works away until we hear the gurgling of water coming from the faucets.

It's as though he keeps himself quiet and calm on purpose.

It's only when he plays his violin that he is a different person. He looks very calm while he's playing, but the music he makes is exciting. When I hear it I can hardly sit still. It fills the house and pours through the windows, sending the birds flying. Grandmama gets a smile on her face and, holding on to my hands, waltzes me around the kitchen.

The song she most often asks Grandpapa to play, though, is a sad one. It's called "*In der Ferne*," "In Far Away Places." "So far away," she sings, "so far away. How I long to be back home."

Grandpapa shakes his head. "You want to go back to a Germany that is no longer there. You would not like today's Germany."

A letter from the Roths finally arrived. It came from Berlin. Grandpapa read a part of it:

We must leave Germany and our home and everything we have. Some of our friends say it will get better, but we are afraid to take a chance. There is a soldier posted in front of our gallery. He warns people not to shop there because we are Jews. Jewish students in the universities have been asked to leave. The labor unions have been shut down. People are afraid to talk on their telephones. We will try to reach Switzerland. From there we hope to get passage on a boat to America. We thank you for your kind offer to find work for us. How hard it is to think we might never be able to go back to our home.

"It will be a miracle if they escape." Grandpapa sighed and picked up his violin again, but the music was sad. There was no dancing to it.

There was trouble in my garden. It'd been one of the dryest Augusts ever. It hadn't rained in nearly two weeks. The snapdragons were hanging their heads, the beans had spots on them, the leaves of the tomato plants were all curled up into fists. I tried to water everything, but you have to carry the water a long way, and the big sprinkling can is heavy. Besides, the sun is scorching hot. I slouched upstairs and shut myself into my bedroom so no one would see me cry.

When I looked out of my window I saw my grandfather and grandmother wearing their big straw hats. They were filling a pail and the big sprinkling can from the pump outside of the kitchen. They carried the water out to my garden. They must have made about ten trips.

After supper I went out to look at my garden. The snapdragons were growing straight up. The tomato leaves had their hands open. When I put my hand on the ground, the earth felt damp.

Canning Day

Tomatoes by the hundreds
roll into the kitchen,
jump into the pots,
slip out of their skins,
crowd into jars,
peer through the glass,
their round baby faces
crying red tears.

All morning Grandmama and Grandpapa and I picked tomatoes. We filled one bushel basket after another. The tomatoes were warm and heavy in our hands. "Just the ripe ones," Grandmama kept calling. Three of the tomatoes from my own garden were ripe. The sun was hot on our backs, and once by mistake I touched a tomato worm as big as ten caterpillars. It looked like a green accordion.

After the tomatoes were picked, Grandpapa went fishing with Mr. Ladamacher. "Canning day," he said and hurried away.

The kitchen might have been a witch's den. Pots of boiling water steamed on the stove. Tomato juice, red as blood, was everywhere. Grandmama looked like a witch with her hair flying out of its neat knot and her face smeared with tomato juice where she had wiped away the sweat.

At first all she said to me was, "*Achtung!* Look out! Don't get in the way." She was busy moving steaming kettles on and off the stove. After a bit she put a pile of scalded tomatoes in front of me. "You can take off the skins," she said. "They come off easy."

The skins just slipped off. While I was undressing the tomatoes, Grandmama told me about the farm her family had when she grew up. "The farm wasn't next to our house like it is in this country. We lived in a village and had to walk out into the country a distance of two miles to get to our farm. It wasn't even much of a farm, only a long strip of land. We grew cabbages and turnips and carrots and potatoes, thick lumpy things that gave us a lot of food for our work. At home we had a root cellar dug into the ground next to our house where we stored the vegetables. They lasted us all winter. We ate every potato, even when spring came and they turned green and tasted bitter.

"Land was hard to come by in the old country. If my

friends could see this garden and orchard they would think we were kings. Remember, Elsa, if you can own your own little piece of land you will be all right."

I began to understand why Grandmama was so happy when she was digging around in the garden. I asked, "Next summer when I come up, can I have a bigger piece of land for my garden?"

"So, you want to come up again next year. I'm glad to hear it." Grandmama smiled.

I grinned, too. Now that I thought about it, I had to admit I was happy, except for Tommy, who was a real nuisance.

Tommy turned up just as Grandmama was cleaning up. The whole kitchen was covered with jars of tomatoes.

"How come you made so many when there are just three of you?" Tommy asked.

"*Ach*, it's not just for us. I make them for all of our children. Food isn't that easy to come by these days."

Tommy gave Grandmama a sly look. "I'll bet they taste real good."

"You can take a jar home with you, Tommy," Grandmama said. "Now go out and play with Elsa while I make supper. I'll call you when it's ready."

"You want to go down the gully?" I asked.

Tommy looked over the edge of the bank. "That's just a ditch. What would you want to go down there for?"

"Well, you can stay here for all I care." I started down. After a minute Tommy followed me.

He looked at the creek. "You got tadpoles," he said. He

reached down into the water. "Gotcha!" he said. He held out a squirming black tadpole. "It's got its legs." It was true. The tadpole had a pair of legs on either side of its tail. Tommy couldn't keep his hands off things. He caught a big toad. He caught a frog. He caught a butterfly and put it in his pocket. He pulled up some snake grass to show how you could make a chain out of it. He turned over the logs to look for skinks, which are like tiny lizards. From the way they skitter away you can tell they don't like to be looked for. He picked up stones and threw them into the creek. He built a dam in the creek with mud and sticks so the water piled up into a little pool.

"You're wrecking this place," I said. "You can just leave."

"You don't own it."

"My grandparents own it."

"Then *they'll* have to tell me to get out."

Furious, I started up the bank just in time to hear Grandmama call us for supper. Tommy must have heard, too, because he was right behind me.

I was so angry I could hardly sit at the same table with him. But when I watched how hungry he was and how quickly he ate his dinner, I stopped feeling so angry.

For the First Time

Yesterday
a snake,
green
as
grass,
coiled
beside
the
blue-
berries.
Today
a foolish
hummingbird
hovering above
my flowered hat.
For the first time I remember
from one happiness to another.

The library in Greenbush is so small that in ten weeks I've just about read all the children's books. I can tell which adult books it's all right for me to check out by the way Miss Walthers smiles or frowns when I take them to the desk. When she frowns she usually says, "Why don't you find something else, dear." The only time she looked startled was when I took out the Sanalac County Road Commissioners' Report. It turned out to be pretty surprising because it talked a lot about snow, and it was hard to believe that Greenbush ever had anything but summer.

A lot of the books I take out are about birds and butterflies and bugs. I like to match up the pictures with the things I see every day. I see a lot. I can't believe I ever thought the country was empty. If you look hard enough there is something everywhere, and it is all surprises. Down in the gully I can watch the water striders skate over the top of the creek. Each strider makes five round shadows, one from its body and four from its legs. There are darners, their green and blue bodies so bright you think they must have lights in them. Once, before he saw me, I saw a muskrat bite off a bundle of grass and swim away with it.

On hot days I put on my bathing suit and sit in the lake with the water right up to my neck. I watch the freighters along the lake's edge. They don't seem to be going anywhere, but when you look away and look back again, they have moved. The gulls sail over me, holding almost still in the air. Everything is busy in a slow way.

In the orchard the branches are so heavy with ripening

fruit that they nearly touch the ground. Some of the pears have fallen off the trees. You can hear the buzz of the wasps that come to eat them.

In my own garden the lettuce and peas have been gone for a long time, but we've had my beans for five different meals. My tomatoes are red and fat. In the big garden the corn that was only a few inches high when I first came is now over my head. Each afternoon Grandmama goes out and fills her apron with enough ears of corn for dinner. As we sit on the back porch shucking corn we can see the rabbits nibbling on the parsley. Grandmama shrugs her shoulders. "The parsley has bolted and is no good anyhow," she says.

Even at night there is something. Last night when we turned on the porch light we saw a flying squirrel glide down from the poplar tree to the bird feeder. And there are things you can hear but can't see, like the owl that hoots in the distance and the crickets singing in the dark.

When I wake up in the morning, I don't think about going home anymore. Instead, I wonder if I will find something new that day, and I'm never disappointed. Even when I walk into Greenbush. Tommy must have told the other children in town that I'm not poison because they talk to me now. There's a girl named Betty who's just my age. We sit on the drugstore steps. I made her a bracelet out of shells. Today she brought her mother's nail polish, and we put it on our nails. The color is Pink Passion. She says Tommy likes me, which is the most disgusting thing I ever heard.

Grandmother

I shadow her, surprised
at what her clever hands can do,
thankful for her silence,
for sometimes when she speaks
her words are sour as
green apples.

She scrubs the sheets
in rainwater
and spreads them on the lawn
to bleach, a field of snow

beneath the summer sun.
Her pansies pool
in deep blue lakes
while lilies sweep above
like soaring gulls
and waves of sweet alyssum
lap the ground.
She gathers fruit

and traps it
in glass jars, rows
of red and yellow lanterns
glowing on the pantry shelves.

Her bread dough swells
and puffs and browns
to perfect loaves,
for everything
my grandmother touches
with her hands
undoes her angry words.

Grandmama has been in an angry mood for two days. This morning she scolded me when she saw the Pink Passion polish on my nails. She snapped at Grandpapa when he was late for breakfast. I don't know why she's so cross. I was about to disappear down into the gully to keep out of her way when I remembered my mother telling me to watch my grandmama's hands. Instead of running off, I decided to spend the day following Grandmama.

She started out in the kitchen making bread dough. White clouds flew up into the air as she shook the flour into a bowl. She stirred so hard the bowl skittered around the table. As she kneaded the dough, she picked it up and slapped it down against the pastry board as if she were angry with it. Finally she threw a towel over it and set it on the warm part of the stove to raise.

It was washing day. Grandmama dipped pails full of water out of the rain barrel. She strained out the little bugs that hatch in the water and boiled it on the stove. When she put soap into it, the suds exploded into foamy bubbles that caught the sun. She emptied some of the sudsy water into a small pan and let me wash the napkins and doilies. She put the washboard into her bucket and scraped the clothes up and down on the board until I thought they would fall apart. They went through the wringer not once or twice but three times! We spread out our washing on the grass where the sun would make it white.

After the wash was done, it was time for the garden. She seemed really angry at the little tufts of green she was yanking out of the flower beds. I asked her what they were. "Crabgrass and chickweed," she said. I saved both of the words.

In the kitchen the bread dough grew until it pushed up the clean white towel that covered it. Grandmama shaped the dough into loaves and let it rise again. Then it went into the oven, and the whole house smelled of fresh baked bread.

After lunch we all picked peaches. I picked the ones on the lowest limbs of the trees. Grandmama reached up into the branches. Grandpapa stood on a stepladder. "Handle the fruit gently," he said. "Peaches bruise easily." One by one we lay the fragrant fruit into a bushel basket. When all the ripe peaches were picked, Grandpapa carried the basket into the kitchen. Grandmama boiled up a kettle of sugar syrup. By dinnertime two dozen jars of gold fruit were lined up on the kitchen table.

We had thick slices of the fresh bread with our dinner. For dessert we ate the peaches that were too ripe to can. The peach juice ran down our chins, and we all laughed. Whatever had made Grandmama angry in the morning had disappeared into the clean clothes and the bread and the garden and the jars of perfect peaches.

That Wild Berries
Should Grow

That wild berries should grow
and fling their thorny shoot
above your head and jail you
while you steal their fruit,
that they should let you go.

I picked blackberries with Grandmama today. I was
used to picking raspberries and gooseberries in the
garden, but the blackberries grow way at the back of the
field. Raspberries and gooseberries grow in neat rows
that Grandpapa keeps trimmed. Blackberries grow in a
tall tangle of briars. The shoots were higher than my head
and covered with thorns that tore my dress and scratched
my arms.

I would have given up, but the berries were so plump and juicy. And they were free—a gift.

We wore straw hats so that our hair wouldn't get snagged and strapped pails around our waists so that our hands would be free to pick the berries. In no time the bottoms of our pails were covered, and the blackberries began to heap up. Our hands were stained purple and so were our mouths. While I picked I could hear Grandmama singing a song. She wrote down the German words for me and told me what they meant:

Mit den Händen: klapp-klapp-klapp,
mit den Füssen: trapp-trapp-trapp,
einmal hin, einmal her,
rund herum—das ist nicht schwer.

Noch einmal das schöne Spiel,
weil es mir so gut gefiel.
Einmal hin, einmal her,
rund herum—das is nicht schwer.

With the hand: clap, clap, clap,
with the foot: tap, tap, tap,
this way once, that way once,
turn around—now that's not hard.

Once again the happy game,
because it feels so good to me.
This way once, that way once,
turn around—now that's not hard.

She pointed me in the direction of a bush where the ripe fruit hung in thick clusters. "Over there, *Liebchen*." *Liebchen* means "sweetheart." It was Grandmama's *kosename*, "cozy name," for me. She seemed so happy that it was hard to remember that sometimes she is cross. Just like the blackberries, I thought, you had to get past the thorns to taste the sweet fruit.

We got home with the blackberries just as Grandpapa returned home from Greenbush. He had gone into town to buy a part for the water pump, which had stopped working. Something went wrong with the pump about every week. Then we had to use water from the rain barrel or drag up pails of water from the lake. "Look what I have," he called to us. He was waving a letter. "It's from Switzerland. Kurt and Ruth are safe. Now we must make plans. They can have one of my apartments." He meant the same apartment building where my parents and aunts and uncles live.

"What about a job, Carl?" Grandmama was heaping the blackberries into a pot to make jam. Even if the world was coming to an end she would still be working.

"I'll call the art school. Both of them could teach. In these hard times there won't be much money, but if things get a little better someday they might have their own art gallery again."

The blackberries and sugar were boiling on the stove. It smelled wonderful. All afternoon Grandmama and Grandpapa made plans for their friends, and at the end of the day, besides all their plans there were thirty-five pints of blackberry jam.

September Storm

I watch the storm unhitch
the yellow leaves
from off the birch,
grab the poplar by its scruff,
toss two helpless
gulls that hover
above the tumbled waves.

I watch the bank
I'd walked upon
crumble like a slice of cake
into the gully's belly.

I know that ground,
I know its fleece of chickweed flowers,
its golden dandelions, its taste of sour sorrel.

I know fall will follow
on the storm
to sweep summer
into the net of my
remembering.

Yesterday while I was packing my things the storm came. It happened so suddenly we weren't ready for it. It didn't start with a few plashes of rain on the sidewalk or a dance on the lake. The sky exploded with flashes and a roar of thunder. The wind threw a fit. A minute later the water came down as if someone were throwing it at us, just as Grandmama throws dishwater on her roses.

We ran through the house shutting windows, but the rain was ahead of us, and we had to mop the floors. When the rain was shut out we stood at the windows watching the show. It was a real roughhouse. The birch tree bent over until its branches swept the ground. Apples, pears, and plums rocketed over the orchard. Along the edge of the bank the ground crumbled away into the gully.

What I couldn't stop looking at was the lake. It was turning itself inside out. It was like someone you love suddenly growing angry. The whitecaps came crashing onto the shore. The water reached farther and farther up onto the beach until even the pump house was threatened. A couple of seagulls were tossed around over the churning water. There wasn't a boat to be seen. I hoped the *Billy Boy* was safe on shore.

Just as we finished our supper, the lights went out. Grandpapa brought out kerosene lamps. "Just like old times," he said. The lamps were bright enough so that you could see, but not bright enough that you could see much. I couldn't read, and Grandmama couldn't sew, but Grandpapa could play his violin. He played for nearly an hour while the wind and rain and thunder carried on outside like the loudest orchestra you ever heard.

This morning when I awoke the sun was dancing on my ceiling. I hurried into my clothes and ran to see what was left of my garden. The snapdragons had laid down and died. The cages had saved my tomato plants, but a lot of the tomatoes had shaken loose. Some of them were still green. "We'll have to throw them away," I said.

"No, no," Grandmama told me. "They won't go to waste. We can make green tomato pickles."

Grandpapa was walking around in the orchard. Branches were scattered everywhere. Fruit that had blown off the trees lay on the ground. I couldn't see Grandpapa's face, but I could see how his shoulders were hunched over. He began putting the fallen fruit into a bushel basket. Grandmama and I helped. This time it was Grandmama who was trying to cheer up Grandpapa. "I was going to make jelly today, anyhow," she said. "Now the fruit has been picked for us."

"By rough hands," Grandpapa said with a sad shake of his head.

When we were finished filling the bushel baskets with the bruised fruit I walked down the stairs past the pump house to the beach. The lake was perfectly calm, but all along the beach were souvenirs from the storm. The huge waves had washed in floats from fishing nets and bits of pink and green and lavender glass worn smooth by the water. It was as though the lake had scattered those pretty things along the beach, like presents. It wanted to show that, in spite of the storm, we were still friends.

Last Look

They have shuttered
the eyes of the cottage,
the dresser drawer
pockets are picked,
in the pump house
the heartbeat has stopped.
All that is left
of the summer
is a bushel of pears
in the trunk of the car.

Beyond the birch tree
is bright water
and the smoke
that I see
at the top
of the lake's
wide blue page
is the freighter's
sooty scrawl,
"Go away and return,
go away and return."

S ummer's over, and I'm going home. Grandmama and Grandpapa and I stood at the end of the driveway watching my parents' car come toward us. When I first came to Greenbush, all I wanted was to go home. Now my parents were coming to take me back to the city, and I almost didn't want to go.

"How healthy you look!" Mom threw her arms around me.

"How tall you've grown!" Dad had a wide grin on his face.

I laughed. "Grandmama and Grandpapa make everything grow!"

I held onto my parents' hands and led them to the orchard. I named all the fruit trees for them: Jonathan, Rome Beauty, Spitzenburg, Mayflower, Elberta, Red Haven, Russetts, Bosc, Bartlett, Damson, and Mirabelle. The trees were like good friends.

I got the saltcellar and took Mom and Dad to my own garden. I showed them how we pick tomatoes right off the vine and eat them still warm from the sun. I gave them the bag of my own beans all ready to take home. "Next year," I said, "Grandmama and Grandpapa promised I could have a bigger garden."

I took them to see the lake. I showed them all the things you could find along the beach. I even made them climb down into the gully. "What did you *do* down here?" Mom asked. "There seem to be a lot of bugs and weeds and things."

"That's why I like it," I said, and I told them the names

of the bugs and weeds.

Grandmama took Mom into the pantry to see the jars of fruit and jam and the green tomato pickles. There was a big box all packed with jars for us to take home. Every time we opened a jar of peaches or tomatoes or blackberry jam I would remember the day Grandmama had made them. Grandpapa had picked us a bushel of pears.

We were just going to have our lunch when Tommy turned up. He always seemed to know when it was time to eat. He brought us a big package. "It's some pickerel," he said. Pickerel is just about the best-tasting fish you can get. "You can take it home with you. It's fresh. We caught it this morning." The fish was wrapped in newspapers and chopped ice like they have at Meyer's Fish House. The newspapers were all wet, and the package was leaking.

Mom took it and held it a little way away from her. "Pickerel is my favorite fish. We'll certainly enjoy this. Thank you so much."

"Who is this very nice young man?" Dad asked. Everyone waited for me to introduce Tommy, so I had to.

"You're probably giving your folks a big dinner," Tommy said, so Grandmama asked him to stay and eat with us. He kicked my shins under the table and I kicked his back. Also he took the last piece of cake on the plate, which isn't polite. He told fibs, too. "My dad and I saw this huge fish that was as big as this whole house. We would have caught it if we had had a cat to tie on our line. Fish that big just eat cats."

"Where do fish get cats to eat in the middle of the lake?" I wanted to know.

"People who want to get rid of their cats and kittens dump them in the lake to drown. It happens all the time."

"It does not! That's a terrible thing to say!" Tommy just shrugged. As he was getting ready to go home, Tommy said, "I'll see you next year."

"Not if I see you first," I said. He punched me in the arm and I punched him back.

In spite of the fact that we had just finished a huge lunch, Grandmama packed a big supper for us to eat in the car. Later in the week my grandparents would leave the cottage for the city, too. Dad and Grandpapa were closing some of the shutters on the windows. Mother and Grandmama were putting sheets on the furniture so it wouldn't get dusty over the winter. The cottage was beginning to look like it was getting ready for ghosts.

Finally it was time to go. Our car was loaded. I hugged Grandmama and Grandpapa. Hard. While my mother and dad were saying good-bye to my grandparents, I slipped away to the front of the house. There was the screen porch. There was my old apple tree. And there, stretching as far as I could see, was the shining lake. I stood watching it a long minute. Then I walked slowly back to the car and climbed in.